PANCAKE DAD!

Ken Gordon

Illustrated by Dorothea Taylor

Pancake Dad
Copyright © 2020 by Ken Gordon

All rights reserved
No portion of this book may be reproduced, stored in a retrieval system, or transmitted in any form by any means—electronic, mechanical, photocopy, recording, or other—except for brief quotations in printed reviews, without prior permission of the author.

First Edition

Paperback ISBN: 978-1-64990-818-6

Dedication

Dedicated to our beautiful granddaughter, Khaliyah, may your life be filled with syrupy sweetness and your table overflow with the world's best pancakes; to KT and Cidnee, my inspirations for creating the world's best pancakes; to Craig and Christopher, two of the most awesome young men in our lives; and to all the Pancake Dads working hard to butter up their kids and make their lives syrupy sweet!

It's Saturday Morning . . .

And, on Saturday mornings, Pancake Dad makes his "world-famous" pancakes for Kristian, Leah, and Griffin.

So, every Saturday the children wake up early and rush to their parents' room to wake up their dad.

"It's Saturday Dad! Get up! Time for pancakes!" exclaim the three kids.
"What time is it?" asks Dad, as he sits up, stretches, and rubs his eyes.

"C'mon Dad! You know what time it is! It's time to make your yummy pancakes" says Leah.

"Pancakes? What in the world are you kids talking about?" teases Dad. "Mom, do you have any idea what they are talking about?" says Dad with a smile.

Not answering, Mom simply looks up and puts the pillow on her head.

"Dad, you know what we are talking about! You always act like you don't! C'mon, let's go make some pancakes," says Kristian, grabbing his father's hand and pulling him towards the door.

"Okay, okay, pancakes it is. But first, we need to thank God for allowing us to wake up this morning! Then we need to brush our teeth, wash our faces, and make up our beds. No pancakes until we do these things. Got it? Okay, so let's kneel and thank our Heavenly Father for a new day."

After making their beds, washing their faces, and brushing their teeth, the three kids hurry back to their parents' room. Once Dad is finished brushing his teeth and washing his face, he grabs his robe and heads towards the bedroom door.

"Wait, Dad, you did not make up *your* bed," teases Leah, as she looks over towards the bed.

"Don't even think about it," comes Mom's voice from under the pillow.

The three kids laugh and follow Pancake Dad out of the room and to the stairs.

"Hmmm, maybe today we will just eat cereal and toast," teases Pancake Dad as he walks down the stairs towards the kitchen.

"No!" scream all three in unison, following closely behind their Dad. "It has to be your world-famous pancakes! We want pancakes! We want pancakes!"

You see, every Saturday, Pancake Dad cooks pancakes for his family. This time is important, as he creates special moments and memories with his children, while allowing Mom time to sleep in and rest.

Dad stands in the middle of the kitchen, next to the island looking around.

"Okay, before we get started, who's ready for our Saturday morning Challenge? Do all of you know your verses?"

"Yeth, thir!" beams Griffin.

"I do!" Leah proclaims proudly.

"Piece of cake, Dad! We're good to go!" says Kristian with a salute. "My scripture is Psalm 139:14 – I praise you God, for I am fearfully and wonderfully made."

"Amen! Yes, all of you are fearfully and wonderfully made! God did not make a mistake when He made anything about you! How you look is exactly how God wants you to look. Everything about you is beautiful, and you are perfect to God, to your mom, and to me! Great job, Kristian!"

"Who's next?" says Dad, looking at Leah.

"My scripture is 1 Corinthians 10:31—Whatever you do, do everything for the glory of God."

"Praise God, Leah! Always do your best in everything you do because you are doing it for God. Whether you are at school, at home, or at church, remember to do your best so you make God happy with you. And, if God is happy with you, your mom and I are happy with you too! Great job, Leah!

"Okay, we saved the best for last. Your turn, Griffy!"

"Yeth, Thir! My scripthur ith Firth John 3 and 23—Love one another."

"To God be the glory! Love one another! Amen! That means God wants us to love everyone no matter how they look, where they live, the color of their skin, or their religious beliefs. God is a god of love, never a God of hate! Great job my little big man!"

"Okay, let's see . . ." says Dad, as he begins looking through cabinets. He then puts a mixing bowl on the counter, reaches into the seasoning cabinet, and pulls out several bottles. "Okay, I have all my ingredients, so come over here next to me."

"Yay!" they all exclaim, as they position themselves next to their dad.

Grabbing a few more items from the refrigerator, Dad pours all of the ingredients into the mixing bowl and hums as he stirs.

"Are there any special requests or do you want me to surprise you?" asks Dad.

"Surprise us! Surprise us!" squeal the children with delight.

"Okay, four orders of Pancake Dad's world-famous pancakes coming up!" exclaims Dad.

"Dad, don't you mean five orders?" insists Leah.

"Ahhh. You are so right!" says Pancake Dad, with a smile. "We can never forget Mom! I stand corrected. Five orders of Pancake Dad's world-famous pancakes coming up."

"Griffy, can you get five eggs from the refrigerator and count them out as you put them in that large green bowl on the counter?" asks Dad.

Griffin dashes to the refrigerator, pulls out the tray of eggs, and puts it on the counter.

"One . . . Two . . . Three . . . Four . . . Five . . ." counts Griffin, as he carefully places each egg in the large green bowl.

"Whose turn is it for bacon duty?"

"It's my turn!" beams Leah, raising her hand.

"Okay, take the pack of bacon on the counter and count out enough bacon for each of us.
Leah, if Griffy gets one piece, you and Kristian get two pieces, Mom gets three pieces, and Dad gets four pieces, how many pieces of bacon will you need?"

Leah thought for a moment.

Pause here and let your children provide the answer before moving on

"Twelve! I need twelve pieces!" says Leah excitedly.

"Leah, you are so smart! You could be the President of the United States, a math professor, or a fighter pilot when you grow up! Always remember, you can do anything you put your mind to. Don't ever let anyone limit who you are or who you can be!"

"Kristian, I need you to get the maple syrup and butter from the refrigerator. After you do that, crack each of the eggs into the large bowl and mix them."

Saturday mornings Pancake Dad spends time with his kids and makes the time educational. During his breakfast routine with his children, he loves to hear their laughter, so he also makes the time fun. He leaves his mobile phone, tablet, and laptop in his office so he can totally focus on his children.

    Kristine, Leah, and Griffin love eating all of the different kinds of pancakes their dad cooks for them each Saturday, but, more than the pancakes, they love spending time cooking with their Dad.

    Sometimes Dad has them learn a new scripture from the Bible or talk about an event going on in the world. This is always a fun time as Kristian, Leah, and Griffin talk into mixing spoons, using them as microphones.

When they are done cooking and having fun, they all rush upstairs to serve Mom breakfast in bed.

Dad reminds the children how important it is to pamper Mom on Saturdays because she works hard all week long.

After serving Mom breakfast, Dad sits at the table and eats breakfast with his children.

During breakfast, Dad asks the children about their friends, their school, and their activities. This is a good time for Dad to learn about all the things his children enjoy and where they are having problems. Dad talks to them about everything and encourages them to share their thoughts and feelings.

No matter what kind of pancakes they cook, Kristian, Leah, and Griffin love Saturday mornings because it is their special time with Dad. And, according to Griffin, "What can be better than thending time with Dad?"

Message to Kids

Kristian 's favorite pancakes are Banana. Leah's favorite pancakes are Cinnamon Nutmeg. Griffin's favorite pancakes are Blueberry.

What are your favorite pancakes? _____
_____

Your favorite kind of pancakes or breakfast is not important. It is not important if your dad makes the same meal every Saturday. What is important is spending time with family, laughing and talking with one another. Your family members are the most important people in the whole wide world. Always love your family because they will always love you.

Message to Dads

Dads, whether you are a great cook or not, set aside Saturday mornings and spend it making breakfast with your children.

Make Saturday mornings their time, with no interruptions. Make it a regular thing your kids can count on. If you cannot cook pancakes as yummy as Pancake Dad's, pick a breakfast you like to cook or want to learn to cook. Then have fun cooking, or learning to cook, with your kids.

Long after they have forgotten the lumps in the grits, the burnt bacon, or the gummy pancakes, they will remember the wonderful times they spent with you in the kitchen!

Remember, it is a Dad's responsibility to create positive memories his kids will remember their entire lives.

Oh, and one more thing . . . while you are cooking with your kids, add generous amounts of hugs and kisses!

Also mix in lots of, "I love yous." and serve them on a daily basis (not just Saturday mornings).

Bon appetite!

Message to Parents

Moms and Dads, my prayer in writing this "Engaged Dad" children's series is that, as parents, we will commit to creating positive, inclusive memories for our children.

With each book in this series, you will notice five (5) common threads, woven throughout.

1. The importance of a dad's engagement with his family, not just his presence in the house or their lives;

2. The importance of a dad modeling manhood (Protector, Provider, and Priest) for his sons;

3. The importance of a dad empowering his daughter, demonstrating how love and respect look, and encouraging her to accept no less;

4. The importance of a dad treating the mother of his children like a queen, whether they are together or not, because she gave him his legacy and the greatest gifts he could ever receive; and

5. The importance of a dad leading his family to a relationship with the Almighty.

I pray you will enjoy reading the books, in this series, to your children and they will enjoy sharing the adventures of Kristian, Leah, and Griffin.

Acknowledgments

Thanks to my Beautiful Angel for providing the spark that turned into "Pancake Dad". Thank you for your creativity, out-of-the-box thinking, and always inspiring me. Thank you to my kids for giving me the inspiration to want to be a great dad. Thanks to my dad for being such a wonderful inspiration and role model.

Thank you Dad for being my "Omelet Dad" and for being just a great Dad!

Thank you to my fabulous illustrator, Dorothea. I am so happy we connected so you could bring my vision of Pancake Dad and his family to life. You captured my vision perfectly. Thank you.

Thank you to my editor. A special thanks to Stephanie with Palmetto Publishing for being the most wonderful, awesome project manager and answering my millions of questions and addressing my millions of changes, with the patience of a saint! Thank you to Logan, Erin, and the entire Palmetto Publishing family for being an incredible, supportive team.

Last, but never last, thanks to God, for without Him, there would be no pancakes!

Other Books in this Series:

Pancake Dad

Pizza Dad

Ice Cream Dad

Date Night Dad

Bible Dad

Homework Dad

Dinner Table Dad

Good Night Dad

Christmas Eve Dad

It's Christmas Dad!

Chore Time Dad

Yard Work Dad

About the Author

Ken Gordon is a father, husband, and author, who has spent many Saturdays in the kitchen making yummy pancakes.

Ken, and his wife Leslie, have four "adulting" children, a beautiful granddaughter, and a chocolate cockapoo puppy.

Now that their children no longer live at home, Ken makes his yummy pancakes for Leslie, whose favorite pancakes are Banana Blueberry Pancakes.

Writing a children's book was Leslie's idea, which she presented to Ken one morning as they were eating pancakes. When she shared the idea, Ken immediately lit up because he believes fathers should spend engaging time with their children, whether it is in the kitchen, playing games at the dining room table, or going out for FroYo.

Printed in the USA
CPSIA information can be obtained
at www.ICGtesting.com
LVHW060934120923
757820LV00004B/12